365 DAYS
OF POETRY PROMISES
AND PRAISE

FOOD FOR YOUR SOUL

LaVerne Montgomery

Unless otherwise indicated all Scripture quotations are taken from the King James Version, © 2003 by Thomas Nelson, Inc. Used by permission.

DEDICATION

365 Days of Poetry Promises and Praise is dedicated to my husband Anthony, who made it possible for me to write this book. Without his love and support I would not have been able to share this gift God has given me.

ACKNOWLEDGEMENTS

I have to thank my Lord and Savior Jesus Christ for using me to get his message of grace and love to others through poetry. God gets the glory for this book, because I trusted solely on his direction, and not my own. I would like to thank photographer, Tony Thaxton Jr. for giving me permission to put one of his beautiful images on this cover. I also want to thank all of my family and friends for giving me feedback on those daily text messages and taking this journey with me. Your positive response lets me know that this book will be a blessing to others as you have been a blessing to me.

Day 1

When we accept the gift of righteousness given through Jesus Christ, it will bless us and our children, more than anything we can buy.

Psalms 115:14

The Lord shall increase you more and more, you and your children.

Day 2

Teach God's promises and provisions so no matter what they face, our children will have assurance of God's everlasting grace.

Isaiah 54:13

And all thy children shall be taught of the Lord; and great shall be the peace of thy children.

Day 3

In darkness there is selfishness, confusion, fear and doubt, but in God's light, love radiates from the inside out.

1 John 1:5

This then is the message which we have heard of him, and declare unto you, that God is light, and in him is no darkness at all.

Day 4

The enemy wants us to be hopeless, to see only what's wrong not right, but God gives us His peace and love, to walk by faith not sight.

2 Timothy 1:7

For God hath not given us the spirit of fear; but of power, and of love, and of a sound mind.

Day 5

God wants to be our only source and solution, but the enemy tries to stop it with distractions and confusion.

1 Corinthians 14:33

For God is not the author of confusion, but of peace, as in all churches of the saints.

Day 6

When we trust God completely, and totally accept his will, He'll make those that come against us, be quiet and still.

Proverbs 16:7

When a man's ways please the Lord, he maketh even his enemies to be at peace with him.

Day 7

Like Jesus, be at peace in the middle of a storm, let the world know
God's got us no matter what is going on.

Psalms 46:10

Be still, and know that I am God: I will be exalted among the heathen,
I will be exalted in the earth.

Day 8

God created us in his image, and gave us authority on this earth, just
like He spoke and saw this world appear, we must speak to give things
birth.

Genesis 1:26

And God said, let us make man in our image, after our likeness; and
let them have dominion over the fish of the sea, and over the fowl of
the air, and over the cattle, and over all the earth, and over every
creeping thing that creepeth upon the earth.

Day 9

Problems in our lives will come and go, but God won't let them overtake us, this I know.

Psalms 41:11

By this I know that thou favourest me, because mine enemy doth not triumph over me.

Day 10

Positive, uplifting and hopeful words, should be spoken to reach our goals. They help us to stay healthy, in our body, mind and soul.

Proverbs 16:24

Pleasant words are as a honeycomb, sweet to the soul, and health to the bones.

Day 11

Before we make tough decisions; pause and ask God about it. He will give us the strength we need, and our steps will be guided.

Psalms 27:14

Wait on the Lord: be of good courage, and he shall strengthen thine heart: wait, I say, on the Lord.

Day 12

God's word will change our heart and mind, if we let it in. When we think and do things differently, the victory begins.

Romans 12:2

And be not conformed to this world: but be ye transformed by the renewing of your mind, that ye may prove what is that good, and acceptable, and perfect, will of God.

Day 13

We should try to think first, before speaking our mind; because we can't take back words, we can't press rewind.

Proverbs 29:11

A fool uttereth all his mind: but a wise man keepeth it in till afterwards.

Day 14

Jesus said passing judgement is a dangerous act, because it will boomerang and come right back.

Matthew 7:1

Judge not, that ye be not judged.

Day 15

Don't let the past create and determine your future.

Philippians 3:13

Brethren, I count not myself to have apprehended: but this one thing I do, forgetting those things which are behind, and reaching forth unto those things which are before.

Day 16

Those who accept the gift of righteousness, are on the path to true wealth. Not just money, but love filled relationships, peace and good health.

Psalms 112:3

Wealth and riches shall be in his house: and his righteousness endureth for ever.

Day 17

God's word affects every part of us; and we should make it our final authority. It teaches and gives wisdom, it's our weapon against the enemy.

Hebrews 4:12

For the word of God is quick, and powerful, and sharper than any two edged sword, piercing even to the dividing asunder of soul and spirit, and of the joints and marrow, and is a discerner of the thoughts and intents of the heart.

Day 18

Spread the word, let God's goodness be told! It makes him happy to see every part of us made whole.

Psalms 35:27

Let them shout for joy, and be glad, that favour my righteous cause: yea, let them say continually, Let the Lord be magnified, which hath pleasure in the prosperity of his servant.

Day 19

Thinking about God's word causes joy inside and out. We get a chance to know that He loves us without a doubt.

Psalms 1:2

But his delight is in the law of the Lord; and in his law doth he meditate day and night.

Day 20

God wants to give us his Holy Spirit; so we will have a helping hand. His word and his Spirit will guide us, that's the master's plan. To receive all of God's promises, some things must be rearranged. Just trust the word and apply it, then we will see a change.

Proverbs 1:23

Turn you at my reproof: behold, I will pour out my spirit unto you, I will make known my words unto you.

Day 21

Don't let negative thoughts get the best of us, keep a positive state of mind. It's beneficial for our health, and a happier life we'll find.

Proverbs 17:22

A merry heart doeth good like a medicine: but a broken spirit drieth the bones.

Day 22

It seems like at times bad guys always win, but God's grace and goodness, is much stronger than sin.

Romans 5:20

Moreover the law entered, that the offence might abound. But where sin abounded, grace did much more abound:

Day 23

When we have a relationship with Jesus, his grace will surround and protect us.

Psalms 5:12

For thou, Lord, wilt bless the righteous; with favour wilt thou compass him as with a shield.

Day 24

Joy comes from what we know; not how we feel. God's promises gives us strength, and faith is our shield.

Nehemiah 8:10

Then he said unto them, Go your way, eat the fat, and drink the sweet, and send portions unto them for whom nothing is prepared: for this day is holy unto our Lord: neither be ye sorry; for the joy of the Lord is your strength.

Day 25

Don't hang out with negative people, run the other way. That negativity will rub off on us, if we decide to stay.

Proverbs 22:24-25

Make no friendship with an angry man; and with a furious man thou shalt not go; Lest thou learn his ways, and get a snare to thy soul.

Day 26

Let's not get overwhelmed by life's issues and problems, God is fighting for us, he knows how to solve them.

2 Chronicles 20:15

And he said, Hearken ye, all Judah, and ye inhabitants of Jerusalem, and thou king Jehoshaphat, Thus saith the Lord unto you, Be not afraid nor dismayed by reason of this great multitude; for the battle is not yours, but God's.

Day 27

God loves us more than we'll ever know, he's holding on to us, even when we let go.

Psalms 37:24

Though he fall, he shall not be utterly cast down; for the Lord upholdeth him with his hand.

Day 28

In this world there is trouble, and danger all around, but protection comes from trusting God, he won't let us down.

Psalms 91:7

A thousand shall fall at thy side, and ten thousand at thy right hand; but it shall not come nigh thee.

Day 29

Praise is our expression of love, for all the world to see. Our hearts are full when we realize, how much God loves you and me.

Psalms 9:1

I will praise thee, O Lord, with my whole heart; I will shew forth all thy marvellous works.

Day 30

The Lord rescues those who are treated unfair. When you trust him, his protection is always there.

Psalms 12:5

For the oppression of the poor, for the sighing of the needy, now will I arise, saith the Lord; I will set him in safety from him that puffeth at him.

Day 31

Faith involves action, not just belief, it is evident in our response to what we feel, hear and see.

James 2:26

For as the body without the spirit is dead, so faith without works is dead also.

Day 32

God wants us to be blessed so just trust and know, we don't have to wait for heaven to see His goodness flow.

Psalms 27:13

I had fainted, unless I had believed to see the goodness of the Lord in the land of the living.

Day 33

Jesus said he would never leave us, that he'd be there all the time. Our outlook on life would change, if we kept this in mind.

Matthew 28:20

Teaching them to observe all things whatsoever I have commanded you: and, lo, I am with you always, even unto the end of the world. Amen.

Day 34

No matter how dark the day is, praise God and enter his presence. It will change how you feel about things, and even your appearance.

Psalms 42:5

Why art thou cast down, O my soul? And why art thou disquieted in me? Hope thou in God: for I shall yet praise him for the help of his countenance.

Day 35

Money is a tool that can be used for good or bad, those loving it more than anything will eventually end up sad.

1 Timothy 6:1

For the love of money is the root of all evil: which while some coveted after, they have erred from the faith, and pierced themselves through with many sorrows.

Day 36

Time is moving at a much slower pace in heaven. What we call a day here, is probably less than a second.

2 Peter 3:8

But, beloved, be not ignorant of this one thing, that one day is with the Lord as a thousand years, and a thousand years as one day.

Day 37

Patience is being at peace in our soul, it doesn't let our thoughts and feelings take control.

Luke 21:19

In your patience possess ye your souls.

Day 38

From Genesis to Revelation God tells us what is to come. His plan is for restoration, and through Jesus it is done.

Isaiah 46:10

Declaring the end from the beginning, and from ancient times the things that are not yet done, saying, My counsel shall stand, and I will do all my pleasure.

Day 39

God promises that he will be a safe haven for us. His help is always available, all we have to do is trust.

Psalms 46:1

God is our refuge and strength, a very present help in trouble.

Day 40

True worship is when your spirit man comes in direct contact with God. At that point anything is possible, nothing is too hard.

John 4:24

God is a Spirit: and they that worship him must worship him in spirit and in truth.

Day 41

Our struggles in life may seem physical, but it's spiritual indeed.
Jesus already defeated the enemy, he is all we really need.

Ephesians 6:12

For we wrestle not against flesh and blood, but against principalities,
against powers, against the rulers of the darkness of this world, against
spiritual wickedness in high places.

Day 42

When we accept the gift of righteousness we take part in the Master's
Plan; to forgive all of our sins, and restore God's relationship with
man.

Ezekiel 33:16

None of his sins that he hath committed shall be mentioned unto him:
he hath done that which is lawful and right; he shall surely live.

Day 43

Jesus wants to be part our lives so it will be easier, not harder. His grace is not meant to weigh you down, but lift you up to the Father.

Matthew 11:30

For my yoke is easy, and my burden is light.

Day 44

Love is never afraid, it casts all fear aside. Being in fear holds us hostage, and is rooted in worry and pride.

1 John 4:18

There is no fear in love; but perfect love casteth out fear: because fear hath torment. He that feareth is not made perfect in love.

Day 45

Beware of those who talk religiously, and say praise the Lord all day; because Christians are recognized by how they treat others, not by what they say.

Matthew 23:28

Even so ye also outwardly appear righteous unto men, but within you are full of hypocrisy and iniquity.

Day 46

When you want to get your way, treating people any way you choose; it may look like you're winning on the outside, but on the inside there's something you lose.

Matthew 16:26

For what is a man profited, if he shall gain the whole world, and lose his own soul? Or what shall a man give in exchange for his soul?

Day 47

Praising God is good for our body, spirit and soul. In his presence we are at peace, uplifted, and made whole.

Psalms 92:1

It is a good thing to give thanks unto the Lord, and to sing praises unto thy name, O most High:

Day 48

Love is the greatest gift, we can experience or give. Pass it on, and it will make a difference, in the life you live.

1 John 4:11

Beloved, if God so loved us, we ought also to love one another.

Day 49

When we fight, we don't need guns to get the victory, we can use the word of God to defeat the enemy.

2 Corinthians 10:4

(For the weapons of our warfare are not carnal, but mighty through God to the pulling down of strongholds;)

Day 50

Your word teaches me what I need to know, and lights the path where I should go.

Psalms 119:105

Thy word is a lamp unto my feet, and a light unto my path.

Day 51

When you get upset, and feel an attitude about to start, ask God to restore your peace, and not let it affect your heart.

Psalms 51:10

Create in me a clean heart, O God; and renew a right spirit within me.

Day 52

When you let Jesus into your heart, you become God's child, royalty. People may not understand your joy and faith, but unmistakable light they'll see.

1 Peter 2:9

But ye are a chosen generation, a royal priesthood, an holy nation, a peculiar people; that ye should shew forth the praises of him who hath called you out of darkness into his marvellous light:

Day 53

The word of God feeds our spirit man and enables us to thrive, just like food is needed for our physical bodies in order to stay alive.

1 Peter 2:2

As newborn babes, desire the sincere milk of the word, that you may grow thereby.

Day 54

You can know the word inside and out, and claim to hear God's voice, but without unconditional love, you're just basically making noise.

1 Corinthians 13:1

Though I speak with the tongues of men and of angels, and have not charity, I am become as sounding brass, or a tinkling cymbal.

Day 55

When we let God lead us, blessings follow wherever we go. It affects us and others, more than we can know.

Deuteronomy 28:2

And all these blessings shall come on thee, and overtake thee, if thou shalt hearken unto the voice of the Lord thy God.

Day 56

Sometimes doing it God's way causes us to feel alone and awkward, but that's when we know we're not following the crowd, so just keep on moving forward.

Matthew 7:14

Because strait is the gate, and narrow is the way, which leadeth unto life, and few there be that find it.

Day 57

Unforgiveness is a dam that blocks the flow of love.

Ephesians 4:32

And be ye kind one to another, tenderhearted, forgiving one another, even as God for Christ's sake hath forgiven you.

Day 58

Love is not weak, but very strong. It takes strength to love when you've been done wrong.

Matthew 5:46

For if ye love them which love you, what reward have ye? Do not even the publicans the same.

Day 59

Thank you Jesus for giving the Holy Spirit to me. You're the bridge that gives me access to God, which is where I want to be.

Ephesians 2:18

For through him we both have access by one Spirit unto the Father.

Day 60

Jesus, your grace is the reason I'm able to please you, your grace is a gift that makes me brand new.

Hebrews 13:21

Make you perfect in every good work to do his will, working in you that which is well pleasing in his sight, through Jesus Christ; to whom be glory for ever and ever. Amen.

Day 61

No matter what it looks like or what the situation may be; when the Lord is with you, blessings and increase will be seen.

Genesis 39:3

And his master saw that the Lord was with him, and that the Lord made all that he did to prosper in his hand.

Day 62

Live your life with integrity, and always do what you say. Trust God's word and promises, because he always makes a way.

1 Corinthians 14:40

Let all things be done decently and in order.

Day 63

Be sure your words and actions are positive and true, because what you put out is multiplied, and comes right back to you.

Hosea 8:7

For they have sown the wind, and they shall reap the whirlwind.

Day 64

Without accepting the gift of salvation and grace, our deeds are not sufficient. Faith is the bridge that connects us to God's favor and provision.

Ephesians 2:8

For by grace are ye saved through faith; and not of yourselves: it is the gift of God.

Day 65

Faith is spiritual material that will manifest what you believe. It is what you hold on to; until physical results can be seen.

Hebrews 11:1

Now faith is the substance of things hoped for, the evidence of things not seen.

Day 66

When you are in a situation and don't know what to do; ask God for directions, he will give it to you.

James 1:5

If any of you lack wisdom, let him ask of God, that giveth to all men liberally, and upbraideth not; and it shall be given him.

Day 67

What you don't know won't hurt you is not necessarily true. You are at risk for being deceived, if you don't know the truth.

Hosea 4:6

My people are destroyed for lack of knowledge.

Day 68

God is always looking out for us so there's nothing that we lack. He goes before us to clear the path and he always has our back.

Psalms 139:5

Thou has beset me behind and before, and laid thine hand upon me.

Day 69

No matter what's going on, talk to God and thank him for his help in advance, even those around you will be affected, and that situation won't have a chance.

Acts 16:25-26

And at midnight Paul and Silas prayed, and sang praises unto God: and the prisoners heard them. And suddenly there was a great earthquake, so that the foundations of the prison were shaken: and immediately all the doors were opened, and every one's bands were loosed.

Day 70

If you believe in your heart that Jesus died for you, when you say it, your spirit will be made brand new.

Romans 10:10

For with the heart man believeth unto righteousness; and with the mouth confession is made unto salvation.

Day 71

Practice getting to know God while things are good for you, so when things get rough, you will know what to do. You won't get bent out of shape when problems occur, because you'll know where to go, you've done it before.

Jeremiah 12:5

If thou hast run with the footman, and they have wearied thee, then how canst thou contend with horses? And if in the land of peace, where in you trusted, they wearied thee, then how wilt thou do in the swelling of Jordan.

Day 72

When things don't seem to go our way, maybe it's connected to what we say.

Proverbs 6:2

Thou art snared with the words of thy mouth, thou art taken with the words of they mouth.

Day 73

Trust God and he will provide, even the needs of your children will be supplied.

Psalms 37:25

I have been young, and now am old; yet have I not seen the righteous forsaken, nor his seed begging bread.

Day 74

Healing is available to all who believe, it is a benefit we all can receive. Physical or emotional, it's all covered in his plan, stake your claim from God's word then on his promise just stand.

Jeremiah 30:17

For I will restore health unto thee, and I will heal thee of thy wounds, saith the Lord;

Day 75

When we believe and accept God's unconditional love for us, doubts will fade away, and be replaced with total trust.

Psalms 145:8

The Lord is gracious, and full of compassion; slow to anger, and of great mercy.

Day 76

We can't make wise decisions without the information we need. The word has the wisdom to help us understand and succeed.

Proverbs 4:7

Wisdom is the principal thing; therefore get wisdom: and with all thy getting get understanding.

Day 77

When we put God first, we won't have to worry about a thing. He will not let us down, all good things he will bring.

Psalms 34:10

The young lions do lack, and suffer hunger: but they that seek the Lord shall not want any good thing.

Day 78

When God's love flows through us, our presence will shine bright. The world will see something different in us, less darkness and more light.

Isaiah 60:2

For, behold, the darkness shall cover the earth, and gross darkness the people: but the Lord shall arise upon thee, and his glory shall be seen upon thee.

Day 79

Expect to win and not to lose, what you think and say, is what you choose.

Proverbs 13:2

A man shall eat good by the fruit of his mouth: but the soul of the transgressors shall eat violence.

Day 80

Don't be upset when crooks always get ahead. Trust God, he will handle it, just be patient instead.

Psalms 37:7

Rest in the Lord, and wait patiently for him: fret not thyself because of him who prospereth in his way, because of the man who bringeth wicked devices to pass.

Day 81

Words don't evaporate, they accumulate.

Isaiah 55:11

So shall my word be that goeth forth out of my mouth: it shall not return unto me void, but it shall accomplish that which I please, and it shall prosper in the thing whereto I sent it.

Day 82

Provision, open doors, and solutions we can expect, because Jesus said when we ask for help, every need will be met.

Matthew 7:7

Ask, and it shall be given you; seek, and ye shall find; knock, and it shall be opened unto you:

Day 83

Thank you Lord for your promises, they always come to pass. Your words don't fail or expire, they always produce and last.

Matthew 24:35

Heaven and earth shall pass away, but my words shall not pass away.

Day 84

The enemy tries to block every blessing with stress. Talk to God, don't shut him out, and you'll experience his best.

Psalms 118:5

I called upon the Lord in distress: the Lord answered me, and set me in a large place.

Day 85

Whatever gift God has given to you, will prosper, because that's what you're meant to do. His will is for us to have joy, and to thrive; to find fulfillment and purpose in our every day lives.

Psalms 128:2

For thou shalt eat the labor of thine hands: happy shalt thou be, and it shall be well with thee.

Day 86

Never be too shy to give God praise; its our way of letting the world know we are thankful for each day.

Psalms 150:6

Let everything that hath breath praise the Lord. Praise ye the Lord.

Day 87

Time to rise and shine, this is what it's all about. The world needs to see something different in us, it's time for God's love to come out.

Isaiah 60:1

Arise, shine, for thy light is come, and the glory of the Lord is risen upon thee.

Day 88

The ability to succeed and excel is what God gives to us, all areas of our lives will be affected, but it begins with trust.

Deuteronomy 8:18

But thou shalt remember the Lord thy God: for it is he that giveth thee power to get wealth, that he may establish his covenant which he sware unto thy fathers, as it is this day.

Day 89

Lord help us see what is right in this world; not only what's wrong; and when we feel like complaining, let us praise you with a song.

Philippians 2:14

Do all things without murmurings and disputings.

Day 90

When you're committed and dedicated to what God called you to do, you will find yourself around people that want to help you.

Proverbs 22:29

Seest thou a man diligent in his business? He shall stand before kings; he shall not stand before mean men.

Day 91

Belief puts you to bed in a place called rest.

Hebrews 4:3

For we which have believed do enter into rest.

Day 92

Even though I don't deserve it, you are always there when I call. Your loving kindness helps me, and lifts me when I fall.

Psalms 94:18

When I said, my foot slippeth; thy mercy, O Lord, held me up.

Day 93

Jesus has made the blessings available to us all, but obstacles and pressures try to make us give up and fall.

Philippians 3:14

I press toward the mark for the prize of the high calling of God in Christ Jesus.

Day 94

It's no problem for God to meet all of our needs. Jesus paid the price, we only have to believe.

Philippians 4:19

But my God shall supply all your need according to his riches in glory by Christ Jesus.

Day 95

When helping others is more important, than what we can get, God has promised to make sure all of our needs will be met.

Luke 6:38

Give, and it shall be given unto you; good measure, pressed down, and shaken together, and running over, shall men give into your bosom. For with the same measure that ye mete withal it shall be measured to you again.

Day 96

You are awesome Lord, and deserving of my praise. I will thank and exalt you for the rest of my days.

Psalms 145:3

Great is the Lord, and greatly to be praised; and his greatness is unsearchable.

Day 97

My heart is full of joy Lord, when I come into your presence. As my mouth speaks your word, on this earth it is established.

Psalms 45:1

My heart is inditing a good matter: I speak of the things which I have made touching the king: my tongue is the pen of a ready writer.

Day 98

It's a blessing to know, that you are with us wherever we go.

1 Corinthians 3:16

Know ye not that ye are the temple of God, and that the Spirit of God dwelleth in you?

Day 99

When the focus is not on us, but what others may need, we will lack nothing, be blessed, and always succeed.

Acts 20:35

I have shewed you all things, how that so laboring ye ought to support the weak, and to remember the words of the Lord Jesus how he said, it is more blessed to give than to receive.

Day 100

I didn't mean that; is something we like to say, when we don't want them to know we really feel that way.

Matthew 12:34

For out of the abundance of the heart, the mouth speaketh.

Day 101

With God on our side, there is promotion and supply. His blessings are eternal, something money can't buy.

Proverbs 8:18

Riches and honour are with me; yea, durable riches and righteousness.

Day 102

We can believe God's word because just like in the beginning, whatever he speaks goes from unseen into being.

Isaiah 46:11

I have spoken it, I will also bring it to pass; I have purposed it, I will also do it.

Day 103

When my path is not clear, and the answers I don't know, your word gives me directions on the best way to go.

Psalms 16:7

I will bless the Lord, who hath given me counsel: my reins also instruct me in the night seasons.

Day 104

When God blesses you, it's like a dream come true.

Psalms 126:1

When the Lord turned again the captivity of Zion, we were like them that dream.

Day 105

When we trust God's direction to bring us increase; we will see blessings that do not cease. But when money is our only goal, it will affect both body and soul.

Proverbs 28:20

A faithful man shall abound with blessings: but he that maketh haste to be rich shall not be innocent.

Day 106

Belief is the key to receive God's provisions. Stay focused on what the word says, not the television.

Matthew 21:22

And all things, whatsoever ye shall ask in prayer, believing, ye shall receive.

Day 107

Following God's lead brings success and open doors. He gives us great ideas, that we can't take credit for.

Isaiah 48:17

Thus saith the Lord, thy Redeemer, the Holy One of Israel; I am the Lord thy God which teacheth thee to profit, which leadeth thee by the way that thou shouldest go.

Day 108

When a believer speaks God's word, it's the language angels understand. They hear it and go into action, to make it manifest for man.

Psalms 103:20

Bless the Lord, ye his angels, that excel in strength, that do his commandments, hearkening unto the voice of his word.

Day 109

God promises to always be there, and answer us when we call. His amazing wisdom and solutions, will leave us in total awe.

Jeremiah 33:3

Call unto me, and I will answer thee, and shew thee great and mighty things, which thou knowest not.

Day 110

Love is a current; affecting our actions and state of mind. It's God's essence that flows to and through us, and is truly divine.

1 John 4: 7-8

Beloved, let us love one another: for love is of God; and every one that loveth is born of God, and knoweth God. He that loveth not knoweth not God; for God is love.

Day 111

Jesus made available to us, his abundant grace, so God would be magnified, and our sins could be erased.

2 Corinthians 12:9

And he said unto me, my grace is sufficient for thee: for my strength is made perfect in weakness.

Day 112

Lord, you protect me from the attacks of the enemy. Your strength and might, wins every fight.

Psalms 61:3

For thou hast been a shelter for me, and a strong tower from the enemy.

Day 113

Lord, on your words and promises I will stand, I trust you more than any man.

Psalms 118:8

It is better to trust in the Lord than to put confidence in man.

Day 114

When the enemy tries to knock me down or take me out; your promise of abundant life, I will boldly shout.

Psalms 118:17

I shall not die, but live, and declare the works of the Lord.

Day 115

Your word is like fresh water to my thirsty soul. Lord with you I bloom and flourish, I'm made completely whole.

Psalms 1:3

And he shall be like a tree planted by the rivers of water, that bringeth forth his fruit in his season; his leaf also shall not wither; and whatsoever he doeth shall prosper.

Day 116

I look to you Lord for guidance and direction, because life is full of unanswered questions.

Proverbs 3: 5-6

Trust in the Lord with all thine heart; and lean not unto thine own understanding. In all thy ways acknowledge him, and he shall direct thy paths.

Day 117

Keep your eyes on the word, they are promises from God. It will protect, guide, and be a source of joy; when things in life get hard.

Proverbs 29:18

Where there is no vision, the people perish: but he that keepeth the law, happy is he.

Day 118

Eternal life and righteousness are not Jesus' only gifts; but we won't expect anything else, if we don't know they exist.

Proverbs 8:21

That I may cause those that love me to inherit substance; and I will fill their treasures.

Day 119

When we have the word inside of us, and Jesus is our Savior, whatever we need will be supplied, whether its minor or major.

John 15:7

If ye abide in me, and my words abide in you, ye shall ask what ye will, and it shall be done unto you.

Day 120

Peace is being able, to trust God's word and rest. When we realize Jesus is with us, there is no need to stress.

Philippians 4:7

And the peace of God, which passeth all understanding, shall keep your hearts and minds through Christ Jesus.

Day 121

God created us to receive his love; we are his family. When we praise him we return his love, with thanksgiving that can be seen.

Isaiah 43:21

This people have I formed for myself; they shall shew forth my praise.

Day 122

If you are in a situation, and don't know what to do, ask God for his guidance, he won't leave or give up on you.

Isaiah 42:16

And I will bring the blind by a way that they knew not; I will lead them in paths that they have not known: I will make darkness light before them, and crooked things straight. These things will I do unto them, and not forsake them.

Day 123

God gave us authority and dominion, to enforce his word. In order to change this world's condition, they must be spoken and heard.

Psalms 115:16

The heaven, even the heavens, are the Lord's: but the earth hath he given to the children of men.

Day 124

God has given us all authority, to use on earth right now. We can't get mad and blame Him, for the things that we allow.

Genesis 1:26

And God said, Let us make man in our image, after our likeness: and let them have dominion over the fish of the sea, and over the fowl of the air, and over the cattle, and over all the earth, and over every creeping thing that creepeth upon the earth.

Day 125

The good news that we should spread each and everyday, is that God's loves can make us whole, and never goes away.

Ephesians 6:15

And your feet shod with the preparation of the gospel of peace.

Day 126

When God blesses his children, he goes overboard. Enemies can't help but acknowledge, our benefits and rewards.

Psalms 23:5

Thou preparest a table before me in the presence of mine enemies: thou anointest my head with oil; my cup runneth over.

Day 127

Jesus when you sacrificed your life for me on that cross; you bought healing for my spirit and body, you paid the ultimate cost.

1 Peter 2:24

Who his own self bare our sins in his own body on the tree, that we, being dead to sins, should live unto righteousness: by whose stripes ye were healed.

Day 128

Lord check me out from head to toe, whatever needs to change, let me know.

Psalms 26:2

Examine me, O Lord, and prove me: try my reins and my heart.

Day 129

When we are honest with God, and ask for his help, he will renew and restore our lives, and it will be well.

1 John 1:9

If we confess our sins, he is faithful and just to forgive us our sins, and cleanse us from all unrighteousness.

Day 130

Prayer is a conversation with God one on one, not just calls for help, when we need something done. If we talk and listen to Him everyday, he will move us or obstacles out of our way.

1 Thessalonians 5:17

Pray without ceasing.

Day 131

When we do things a certain way because it was done like that before; no results will be seen from the word, because we trust in our ways more.

Mark 7:13

Making the word of God of none effect through your tradition, which ye have delivered: and many such like things do ye.

Day 132

Food doesn't make you unclean; that's not where it starts. It comes from the inside not outside; what corrupts a man is his heart.

Mark 7:15

There is nothing from without a man, that entering into him can defile him: but the things which come out of him, those are they that defile the man.

Day 133

Your whole being is in sync with God when you allow His love to flow. It will cause your outlook on life to change, and your capacity to love will grow; then the tides will turn in your favor, and victory you will know.

Isaiah 60:5

Then thou shalt see, and flow together, and thine heart shall fear, and be enlarged; because the abundance of the sea shall be converted unto thee, the forces of the Gentiles shall come unto thee.

Day 134

Lord you know me inside and out, so I won't live in fear, You watch over and protect me, more than the birds in the air.

Luke 12:7

But even the very hairs of your head are all numbered. Fear not therefore: ye are of more value than many sparrows.

Day 135

God's word is a force that can handle anything, it will demolish any problem that the enemy may bring.

Jeremiah 23:29

Is not my word like as a fire? saith the Lord; and like a hammer that breaketh the rock in pieces.

Day 136

Doing the right thing, and being honest, affects you and your children too. There will be blessings and success, because of what you do.

Proverbs 20:7

The just man walketh in his integrity: his children are blessed after him.

Day 137

For the believer, angels are the CIA; they are Covenant In forcing Angels to help us each day. They protect and serve the children of God, they are all around us doing their job.

Psalms 91:11

For he shall give his angels charge over thee, to keep thee in all thy ways.

Day 138

Lord you want the very best for us, because you are love. You'll never hurt, or put us down, because that's not what love does.

Jeremiah 24:6

For I will set mine eyes upon them for good, and I will bring them again to this land: and I will build them, and not pull them down; and I will plant them, and not pluck them up.

Day 139

When we ask for help with a sincere heart, God steps right in, because he is never far.

Psalms 145:18

The Lord is nigh unto all them that call upon him, to all that call upon him in truth.

Day 140

When we trust the Lord completely, we live in the over and above; we can't help but thank and praise him, for uplifting us with his love.

Joel 2:26

And ye shall eat in plenty, and be satisfied, and praise the name of the Lord your God, that hath dealt wondrously with you: and my people shall never be ashamed.

Day 141

A smart person knows how to use their words effectively to teach, but wisdom knows that how we say it, is more important than what we speak.

Proverbs 16:21

The wise in heart shall be called prudent: and the sweetness of the lips increaseth learning.

Day 142

When our spirit is connected to God, our body can overcome illness, but without that connection, our spirit is weak, and our body becomes defenseless.

Proverbs 18:14

The spirit of a man will sustain his infirmity; but a wounded spirit who can bear.

Day 143

When we can't control our emotions, we leave ourselves open to the enemy. We will say or do something we regret, and taking it back is not easy.

Proverbs 25:28

He that hath no rule over his own spirit is like a city that is broken down, and without walls.

Day 144

With your Holy Spirit guiding me Lord, no problem is too big. I know I have the victory, with you I always win.

1 John 4:4

Ye are of God, little children, and have overcome them: because greater is he that is in you, than he that is in the world.

Day 145

God is always looking out for us, he's ready to clear our path. He can take care of any situation; we just need to ask.

Isaiah 45:2

I will go before thee, and make the crooked places straight: I will break in pieces the gates of brass, and cut in sunder the bars of iron:

Day 146

The word of God is sustenance for our spirit and soul. Food is needed for our bodies to live, but God's word will make us whole.

Matthew 4:4

But he answered and said, It is written, Man shall not live by bread alone, but by every word that proceedeth out of the mouth of God.

Day 147

Jesus is our Savior, protector, helper and friend. He gave his life so we could be righteous, he's with us till the end.

Jude 24

Now unto him that is able to keep you from falling, and to present you faultless before the presence of his glory with exceeding joy.

Day 148

When you are known for deeds that are not good, but bad; people won't trust you, no matter how much you have. Being trustworthy is priceless and worth much more, because it will lead to promotion and open doors.

Proverbs 22:1

A good name is rather to be chosen than great riches, and loving favor rather than silver and gold.

Day 149

Under God's grace we are always forgiven, but that's no excuse to just keep on sinning. Playing the grace card is not a good defense, because with every action, there's a consequence.

1 Corinthians 6:12

All things are lawful unto me, but all things are not expedient: all things are lawful for me, but I will not be brought under the power of any.

Day 150

Don't get discouraged if progress is slow, cheer up God is with you, it will surely grow.

Zechariah 4:10

For who hath despised the day of small things? for they shall rejoice, and shall see the plummet in the hand of Zerubbabel with those seven; they are the eyes of the Lord, which run to and fro through the whole earth.

Day 151

When life tries to weigh us down with stress, worry and fear. Jesus said he will give us rest, those burdens he will bear.

Matthew 11:28

Come unto me, all ye that labor and are heavy laden, and I will give you rest.

Day 152

God's unconditional love can change the heart of a man, when he realizes that it never stops, and that He's our biggest fan.

Jeremiah 31:3

The Lord hath appeared of old unto me, saying, Yea, I have loved thee with an everlasting love: therefore with lovingkindness have I drawn thee.

Day 153

Lord thank you for our benefits package that comes with loving you, unlimited forgiveness and total healing, just to name a few.

Psalms 103:2-3

Bless the Lord, O my soul, and forget not all his benefits: Who forgiveth all thine iniquities; who healeth all thy diseases;

Day 154

When I get confused, and my emotions start running wild; your word gets me back on track, and reminds me that I'm your child.

Psalms 23:3

He restoreth my soul: he leadeth me in the paths of righteousness for his name's sake.

Day 155

Wherever I go, whatever I do, I will always find time to praise and thank you.

Psalms: 100:4

Enter into his gates with thanksgiving, and into his courts with praise: be thankful unto him, and bless his name.

Day 156

Jesus came to build us up, not to tear us down. He wants to give us a fresh start, and turn our lives around.

Luke 9:56

For the Son of Man is not come to destroy men's lives, but to save them.

Day 157

Every day is a gift from God that we should celebrate. When we start out with a positive mindset, each day can be great.

Psalms 118:24

This is the day which the Lord hath made; we will rejoice and be glad in it.

Day 158

What is in my heart, I will eventually say, Lord help my thoughts and words, be a reflection of your ways.

Psalms 19:14

Let the words of my mouth, and the meditation of my heart, be acceptable in thy sight, O Lord, my strength, and my redeemer.

Day 159

When we trust God we live longer, because it alleviates stress; knowing that he is with us, allows our mind and body to rest.

Proverbs 9:11

For by me thy days shall be multiplied, and the years of thy life shall be increased.

Day 160

God knows your limits, and what you can take; when you are tested, a way out he will make.

1 Corinthians 10:13

There hath no temptation taken you but such as is common to man: but God is faithful, who will not suffer you to be tempted above that ye are able; but will with the temptation also make a way to escape, that ye may be able to bear it.

Day 161

God's love for us will never fade away, no matter what happens, his mercy remains.

Malachi 3:6

For I am the Lord, I change not; therefore ye sons of Jacob are not consumed.

Day 162

Sometimes our love is conditional, and changes from day to day, but Jesus' love is constant; it always remains the same.

Romans 8:39

Nor height, nor depth, nor any other creature, shall be able to separate us from the love of God, which is in Christ Jesus our Lord.

Day 163

When we come together in worship and prayer, Jesus said he will be right there.

Matthew 18:20

For where two or three are gathered together in my name, there am I in the midst of them.

Day 164

When we find ourselves in over our head, with no solution in sight; remember we have God on our side, and he's never lost a fight.

2 Chronicles 20:15

And he said, Hearken ye, all Judah, and ye inhabitants of Jerusalem, and thou king Jehoshaphat, Thus saith the Lord unto you, Be not afraid nor dismayed by reason of this great multitude; for the battle is not yours, but God's.

Day 165

When we accept Jesus, and the righteousness he gives, our spirits are awakened, and a new life we will live.

Colossians 3:10

And have put on the new man, which is renewed in knowledge after the image of him that created him:

Day 166

Jesus came to give us the gift of liberty; no more guilt or bondage, we are totally free.

John 8:36

If the Son therefore shall make you free, ye shall be free indeed.

Day 167

There's no need to be afraid of what people may do, you are fully protected, when you have God with you.

Psalms 118:6

The Lord is on my side; I will not fear: what can man do unto me?

Day 168

It doesn't make sense to know it all's when it comes to believing God; they rely only on their own intellect, trusting is too hard.

1 Corinthians 1:27

But God hath chosen the foolish things of the world to confound the wise; and God hath chosen the weak things of the world to confound the things which are mighty;

Day 169

I give God all the glory and praise, my life has changed in amazing ways.

Psalms 118:23

This is the Lord's doing; it is marvellous in our eyes.

Day 170

When I go to sleep God's protection is there; while my body is resting I'm under his care.

Psalms 4:8

I will both lay me down in peace, and sleep: for thou, Lord, only makest me dwell in safety.

Day 171

Trust God and don't forget, he created all things. He will never leave you stranded, his love is everlasting.

Psalms 20:7

Some trust in chariots, and some in horses: but we will remember the name of the Lord our God.

Day 172

God has a plan for your life, and it's full of many good things, he wants all of your dreams to come true, with nothing broken or missing.

Jeremiah 29:11

For I know the thoughts that I think toward you, saith the Lord, thoughts of peace, and not of evil, to give you an expected end

Day 173

Following God's plan gives us peace, even when times are tough.
Without him there is worry, stress, and a path that's twisted and rough.

Isaiah 48:22

There is no peace, saith the Lord, unto the wicked.

Day 174

When all of your thoughts are negative, your mind is under attack.
Think on things more positive, and that's what you will attract.

Philippians 4:8

Finally, brethren, whatsoever things are true, whatsoever things are honest, whatsoever things are just, whatsoever things are pure, whatsoever things are lovely, whatsoever things are of good report; if there be any virtue, and if there be any praise, think on these things.

Day 175

To prosper in life means much more, than just having wealth; it's peace of mind, with loving relationships and also good health.

3 John 1:2

Beloved, I wish above all things that thou mayest prosper and be in health, even as thy soul prospereth.

Day 176

God will never take back his promises, or like man; lie to you. You can be assured that whatever he said, he will surely do.

Numbers 23:19

God is not a man, that he should lie; neither the son of man, that he should repent: hath he said, and shall he not do it? or hath he spoken, and shall he not make it good.

Day 177

We are made righteous by Jesus, we are not what we do, our mind and body must adjust from the old ways to the new.

2 Corinthians 5:17

Therefore if any man be in Christ, he is a new creature: old things are passed away; behold, all things are become new.

Day 178

When the enemy tries to fill your mind with doubt, fear and worry; stand on this word, use your authority, and he will leave in a hurry.

James 4:7

Submit yourselves therefore to God. Resist the devil, and he will flee from you.

Day 179

When your life seems out of order, and you don't know where to start, take time to reflect on how to change the condition of your heart.

Proverbs 4:23

Keep thy heart with all diligence; for out of it are the issues of life.

Day 180

Sometimes we don't understand, but just keep on trusting God. He knows what's in everyone's heart, judging is his job.

Psalms 75:7

But God is the judge: he putteth down one, and setteth up another.

Day 181

Darkness is the enemy's camp, that's filled with fear and doubt; but when you have Jesus with you, his light will lead you out.

Psalms 18:28

For thou wilt light my candle: the Lord my God will enlighten my darkness.

Day 182

All we have to do is look around and see, God's beauty in all of its majesty.

Psalms 19:1

The heavens declare the glory of God; and the firmament sheweth his handiwork.

Day 183

When God is with you people notice, because they see a difference,
an inner peace that shines right through and changes your appearance.

1 Kings 10:1

And when the queen of Sheba heard of the fame of Solomon concerning the name of the Lord, she came to prove him with hard questions.

Day 184

Peace from Jesus is eternal, it lasts even when things aren't right; but
peace from the world is temporary, and can disappear in one night.

John 14:27

Peace I leave with you, my peace I give unto you; not as the world
giveth, give I unto you. Let not your heart be troubled, neither let it be
afraid.

Day 185

Distractions and playing on our emotions, are the enemy's way, of getting us not to trust God, and eventually turn away. He knows that when we see the light, of God's love and believe, all of His goodness and promises, we will receive.

2 Corinthians 4:4

In whom the god of this world hath blinded the minds of them which believe not, lest the light of the glorious gospel of Christ, who is the image of God, should shine unto them.

Day 186

When we get angry, the gift of righteousness gets blocked; but with love and forgiveness, the flow is restored and unlocked.

James 1:20

For the wrath of man worketh not the righteousness of God.

Day 187

People may change from day to day, but Jesus' unconditional love will always stay.

Hebrews 13:8

Jesus Christ the same yesterday, and today, and forever.

Day 188

Don't just hear God's word and promises, make it part of your daily routine; apply them to your everyday life, then those promises will be seen.

James 1:22

But be ye doers of the word, and not hearers only, deceiving your own selves.

Day 189

The enemy wants to destroy us, and drag us through the dirt; but he can't attack us without an opening, so be sure to stay alert.

1 Peter 5:8

Be sober, be vigilant; because your adversary the devil, as a roaring lion, walketh about, seeking whom he may devour.

Day 190

Don't worry or lose sleep over things we can't change, just give it to God who loves us, and watch things rearrange.

1 Peter 5:7

Casting all your care upon him; for he careth for you.

Day 191

God's word is spiritual material; he used it to make this earth. When we believe and stand on his word, we can speak things and give it birth.

Hebrews 11:3

Through faith we understand that the worlds were framed by the word of God, so that the things which are seen were not made of things which do appear.

Day 192

It's hard work to be still, and let God work things out. When we do things on our own, to Him it looks like doubt.

Hebrews 4:11

Let us labor therefore to enter into that rest, lest any man fall after the same example of unbelief.

Day 193

Don't worry about anything, just take it to God in prayer. Give thanks in advance because you know, his help is always there.

Philippians 4:6

Be careful for nothing; but in everything by prayer and supplication with thanksgiving let your requests be made known unto God.

Day 194

Trying to do the right thing, can be very hard sometimes; but remember you are not alone, you have God as your guide.

Philippians 2:13

For it is God which worketh in you both to will and to do of his good pleasure.

Day 195

Spending time in God's word will make us feel brand new. It's refreshing and informative, to get his point of view.

Ephesians 5:26

That he might sanctify and cleanse it with the washing of water by the word.

Day 196

The price has been paid, the reservations are made, you need only accept Jesus' upgrade.

Ephesians 2:6

And hath raised us up together, and made us sit together in heavenly places in Christ Jesus.

Day 197

When nothing seems to be going right, and all you see is a mess, look through your faith glasses, stand on God's word, and let him do the rest.

2 Corinthians 5:7

For we walk by faith, not by sight.

Day 198

When someone gets what you want, don't get mad, or be upset; celebrate with them and be happy; you just might be next.

Romans 12:15

Rejoice with them that do rejoice, and weep with them that weep.

Day 199

Be committed and dedicated to whatever you do, because your work is a mirror reflection of you.

Romans 12:11

Not slothful in business; fervent in spirit serving the Lord.

Day 200

We can't have faith in something, that we never heard. Share the good news of God's love, through his amazing word.

Romans 10:17

So then faith cometh by hearing, and hearing by the Word of God.

Day 201

Adam was responsible for the first sin and fall, but Jesus made righteousness, available to us all.

Romans 5:19

For as by one man's disobedience many were made sinners, so by the obedience of one shall many be made righteous.

Day 202

Talk about God's promises, instead of the problems we see; then watch as they manifest themselves, with the words we speak.

Romans 4:17

(As it is written, I have made thee a father of many nations,) before him whom he believed, even God, who quickeneth the dead, and calleth those things which be not as though they were.

Day 203

Belief in what Jesus did for us, is all we need to be righteous. It can't be worked for or earned, it's a gift that his blood purchased.

Galatians 3:6

Even as Abraham believed God, and it was accounted to him for righteousness.

Day 204

Jesus said there would be some rough times, but there's no need to fear. He has already conquered the enemy, and his protection will always be there.

John 16:33

These things I have spoken unto you, that in me ye might have peace. In the world ye shall have tribulation: but be of good cheer; I have overcome the world.

Day 205

Either you're with me or not; is what Jesus said. There's no neutral ground in faith, it's time to move ahead.

Luke 11:23

He that is not with me is against me: and he that gathereth not with me scattereth.

Day 206

When we believe in Jesus, and his grace that's available; we have access to everything, and anything is possible.

Mark 9:23

Jesus said unto him, If thou canst believe, all things are possible to him that believeth.

Day 207

When we choose God's way of doing things first, and not as a last resort, what we need will be provided, and on top of that, so much more.

Matthew 6:33

But seek ye first the kingdom of God, and his righteousness; and all these things shall be added unto you.

Day 208

Worrying won't solve a problem, it only magnifies it. It doesn't make you feel any better, and can even make you sick.

Matthew 6:27

Which of you by taking thought can add one cubit unto his stature.

Day 209

When we trust God completely, and keep our focus on him, we don't have to toss and turn with worry, because we'll have peace within.

Isaiah 26:3

Thou wilt keep him in perfect peace, whose mind is stayed on thee: because he trusteth in thee.

Day 210

Jealousy is a raging emotion that makes you hot with anger.
It's a joyless feeling that often backfires, and places you in danger.

Song of Solomon 8:6

Set me as a seal upon thine heart, as a seal upon thine arm: for love is strong as death; Jealousy is cruel as the grave: the coals thereof are coals of fire, which hath a most vehement flame.

Day 211

When people plan to make others fall, and enjoy seeing them down; they don't realize that they set themselves up, because it almost always rebounds.

Proverbs 26:27

Whoso diggeth a pit shall fall therein: and he that rolleth a stone, it will return upon him.

Day 212

God has given us power and authority, with the words that we speak; positive words yield victory, complaining yields defeat.

Proverbs 18:21

Death and life are in the power of the tongue: and they that love it shall eat the fruit thereof.

Day 213

When God makes a way for you to have something, it gives you peace, not stress. The provisions to keep it will be there, that's what it means to be blessed.

Proverbs 10:22

The blessing of the Lord, it maketh rich, and he addeth no sorrow with it.

Day 214

God promises us a restful sleep with no need for self medication. It happens when we replace fear with faith, and trust him, without hesitation.

Proverbs 3:24

When thou liest down, thou shalt not be afraid: yea, thou shalt lie down, and thy sleep shall be sweet.

Day 215

God promises that when we need him, he won't let us down. He will come to the rescue, and promote us; his love always abounds.

Psalms 91:15

He shall call upon me, and I will answer him: I will be with him in trouble; I will deliver him, and honour him.

Day 216

When the storms of life are raging, and you feel like you're about to drown; trust and focus on God's protection, he will never let you down.

Psalms 91:2

I will say of the Lord, He is my refuge and my fortress: my God; in him will I trust.

Day 217

When we are happy to be in God's presence, and look forward to being with him; he will make all our dreams come true, each and every one of them.

Psalms 37:4

Delight thyself also in the Lord; and he shall give thee the desires of thine heart.

Day 218

We are not alone on this journey, God is with us all the way. When we ask him, he will show and guide us, to victory each day.

Psalms 25:4

Shew me thy ways, O Lord; teach me thy paths.

Day 219

I'm on solid ground with Jesus, he's my safety net when I fall; my relationship with God isn't a tightrope, with no room for mistakes at all.

Psalms 18:36

Thou hast enlarged my steps under me, that my feet did not slip.

Day 220

God wants us to know we are never alone. He's a father that wants his children to come home. Through him there is victory; he will lift us up for all to see.

1 Chronicles 29:12

Both riches and honour come of thee, and thou reignest over all; and in thine hand is power and might; and in thine hand it is to make great, and to give strength unto all.

Day 221

When you speak and focus on God's word, it becomes a part of you; and soon you will find joy and success, in every thing you do.

Joshua 1:8

This book of the law shall not depart out of thy mouth; but thou shalt meditate therein day and night, that thou mayest observe to do according to all that is written therein: for then thou shalt make thy way prosperous, and then thou shalt have good success.

Day 222

God's wisdom gives us the answers we need; it even enables our children to succeed.

Deuteronomy 29:29

The secret things belong unto the Lord our God: but those things which are revealed belong unto us and to our children forever, that we may do all the words of this law.

Day 223

God always gives us a choice, and he wants us to choose him; but it has to be our decision, to let his favor and mercy come in.

Deuteronomy 30:19

I call heaven and earth to record this day against you, that I have set before you life and death, blessing and cursing: therefore choose life, that both thou and thy seed may live.

Day 224

When we accept Jesus as our savior; we become part of God's family. There's nothing we can do to earn it, because a gift is just received.

Galatians 3:26

For ye are all the children of God by faith in Christ Jesus.

Day 225

God's word is still relevant, and can be applied to our lives today; its not like the things on this earth, that will eventually pass away.

Isaiah 40:8

The grass withereth, the flower fadeth,: but the word of our God shall stand forever.

Day 226

When people are divided, there's no progress or harmony. The enemy uses this tactic, to destroy nations and families.

Mark 3:25

And if a house be divided against itself, that house cannot stand.

Day 227

A jealous and complaining person will see more wrong than right. The enemy wants life to feel hopeless; and that's his way inside.

James 3:16

For where envying, and strife is, there is confusion and every evil work.

Day 228

Praise is a powerful weapon, that calls the Lord to our side. Those against us won't have a chance, because from God, there's nowhere to hide.

2 Chronicles 20:22

And when they began to sing and praise, the Lord set ambushments against the children of Ammon, Moab, and Mount Seir; which were come against Judah; and they were smitten.

Day 229

I praise and thank you all day Lord, because each morning you open my eyes; you watch over me throughout the day, and bring me home safely each night.

Psalms 113:3

From the rising of the sun unto the going down of the same the Lord's name is to be praised.

Day 230

My life is filled with joy, because I know you for myself, it's not based on what I have, my status or my wealth.

Psalms 4:7

Thou has put gladness in my heart, more than in the time that their corn and their wine increased.

Day 231

Charity is simply love for one another. It's caring and doing for our sisters and brothers. Love, hope and faith are all qualities to possess, but God is love; which makes it bigger than the rest.

1 Corinthians 13:13

And now abideth faith, hope, charity, these three, but the greatest of these is charity.

Day 232

God's plan to save and repair, what's broken in our lives; was revealed and put into action, when Jesus arrived.

Ezekiel 36:33

Thus saith the Lord God; In the day that I shall have cleansed you from all your iniquities I will also cause you to dwell in the cities, and the wastes shall by builded.

Day 233

There's a place for us in heaven, when this life is through. Our bodies are just temporary, we are spirits in earth suits.

2 Corinthians 5:1

For we know that if our earthly house of this tabernacle were dissolved, we have a building of God, an house not made with hands, eternal in the heavens.

Day 234

Jesus came to restore us to a sin free state, back to a relationship with our Father, and a fresh clean slate.

2 Corinthians 5:21

For he hath made him to be sin for us, who knew no sin; that we might be made the righteousness of God in him.

Day 235

There is nothing too hard for God to do, all he requires is total trust from you.

Jeremiah 32:27

Behold, I am the Lord, the God of all flesh: is there anything too hard for me?

Day 236

You put yourself in a position, to lose and not receive, when you hold back and decide, not to help someone in need.

Proverbs 11:24

There is that scattereth, and yet increaseth; and there is that withholdeth more than is meet, but it tendeth to poverty.

Day 237

God said he will always be on our side, when trouble comes, no need to hide. If we trust him and follow his lead, we will be shining examples of how to succeed.

Psalms 50:15

And call upon me in the day of trouble: I will deliver thee, and thou shalt glorify me.

Day 238

We all have a purpose, when God created us he knew, that if we let him in our hearts, his love would shine right through.

Isaiah 43:7

Even every one that is called by my name: for I have created him for my glory, I have formed him; yea I have made him.

Day 239

We call our fathers by different names like Daddy, Papi, and Pop. Why do we fight over what we call God? This has got to stop.

Ephesians 4:6

One God and Father of all, who is above all, and through all, and in you all.

Day 240

Those who don't believe, will see how God turns things around. He always does what he says, no matter how impossible it sounds.

Ezekiel 36:36

Then the heathen that are left round about you shall know that I the Lord build the ruined places, and plant that that was desolate: I the Lord have spoken it, and I will do it.

Day 241

To find our purpose in life, just trust God and follow his lead. He created us for a reason, and knows what we're meant to be.

Jeremiah 17:7

Blessed is the man that trusteth in the Lord, and whose hope the Lord is.

Day 242

Angels are on duty day and night, they don't let God's children out of their sight. Their assignment is to protect and defend, those who put their trust in Him.

Psalms 34:7

The angel of the Lord encamps round about them that fear him, and delivereth them.

Day 243

Trusting God will lead, to blessings people see.

Psalms 34:8

O taste and see that the Lord is good: blessed is the man that trusteth in him.

Day 244

When we are confused and don't have a clue, Gods wisdom sheds light on what to do.

Psalms 112:4

Unto the upright there ariseth light in the darkness: he is gracious, and full of compassion, and righteous.

Day 245

Jesus came to restore us, and to make our lives complete, but the enemy wants us discouraged, and living in defeat.

John 10:10

The thief cometh not, but for to steal, and to kill, and to destroy: I am come that they might have life, and that they have it more abundantly.

Day 246

When problems try to overwhelm us, don't worry or get confused; just know God will help us solve them, so there's no need for the blues.

2 Corinthians 4:8

We are troubled on every side, yet not distressed; we are perplexed, but not in despair;

Day 247

It may look like we are aging and our bodies are getting weak, but the real strength lies in our spirit, it's more important than what you see.

2 Corinthians 4:16

For which cause we faint not; but though our outward man perish, yet the inward man is renewed day by day.

Day 248

We may go through some things as a child of God, but He promises us a way out; no problem is too hard.

Psalms 34:19

Many are the afflictions of the righteous; but the Lord delivereth him out of them all.

Day 249

The gift of righteousness is protection, for our heart from guilt and shame. The truth is Jesus paid the price for our sins; that is why he came.

Ephesians 6:14

Stand therefore, having your loins girt about with truth, and having on the breastplate of righteousness.

Day 250

When we teach the word to our children, we may not see results right away; but as they grow it will guide them, and help them from going astray.

Proverbs 22:6

Train up a child in the way he should go: and when he old, he will not depart from it.

Day 251

God will always cause us to come out on top, if we listen and follow his lead. His word puts us ahead in life, and enables us to succeed.

Deuteronomy 28:13

And the Lord shall make thee the head, and not the tail; and thou shalt be above only, and thou shalt not be beneath; if that thou hearken unto the commandments of the Lord thy God, which I command thee this day, to observe and to do them.

Day 252

When we make God a part of our lives, he brings peace instead of gloom. We are happy and full of praise because, what was withered is now in bloom.

Isaiah 51:3

For the Lord shall comfort Zion: he will comfort all her waste places; and he will make her wilderness like Eden, and her desert like the garden of the Lord; joy and gladness shall be found therein, thanksgiving, and the voice of melody.

Day 253

When someone treats you wrong, don't retaliate with the same. Maintain a position of inner peace, because your blessing is on the way.

1 Peter 3:9

Not rendering evil for evil, or railing for railing: but contrariwise blessing; knowing that ye are thereunto called, that ye should inherit a blessing.

Day 254

A positive word brings happiness to all those who hear; when it's said at the right time, it's like a breath of fresh air.

Proverbs 15:23

A man hath joy by the answer of his mouth: and a word spoken in due season, how good is it!

Day 255

Food is needed for my body to survive, but your word causes my soul and spirit to thrive.

Job 23:12

Neither have I gone back from the commandment of his lips; I have esteemed the words of his mouth more than my necessary food.

Day 256

When I focus on you Lord, your goodness I see. Blessings and favor are in hot pursuit of me.

Psalms 23:6

Surely goodness and mercy shall follow me all the days of my life: and I will dwell in the house of the Lord for ever.

Day 257

God wants his love to flows through us, that's the Master's plan. We illustrate his love, when it's shown to our fellow man.

Romans 13:10

Love worketh no ill to his neighbor: therefore love is the fulfilling of the law.

Day 258

God is waiting patiently, for all of us to come home. He wants to be a part of our lives; we don't have to go it alone.

2 Peter 3:9

The Lord is not slack concerning his promise, as some men count slackness; but is longsuffering to us-ward, not willing that any should perish, but that all should come to repentance.

Day 259

Thank you Lord for your mercy, it doesn't give us what we deserve .
Your endless supply never runs out; for us it has been reserved.

Psalms 136:1

O give thanks unto the Lord; for he is good: for his mercy endureth
for ever.

Day 260

Lord, you create with the words you speak. Thank you for what you
did in just one week.

Psalms 148:5

Let them praise the name of the Lord: for he commanded, and they
were created.

Day 261

When we are out of options, and think it can't be done, God can make a way when there seems to be none.

Luke 1:37

For with God nothing shall be impossible

Day 262

Jesus took the blinders off, and lit a path in the dark. He broke the enemy's hold on us and gave us a brand new start.

Acts 26:18

To open their eyes, and to turn them from darkness to light, and from the power of Satan unto God, that they may receive forgiveness of sins, and inheritance among them which are sanctified by faith that is in me.

Day 263

I'm all in Lord, it's settled; there is no changing my mind. I rejoice because I trust you with every part of my life .

Psalms 57:7

My heart is fixed, O God, my heart is fixed: I will sing and give praise.

Day 264

The word of God is wisdom, filled with promises I can find. It shows me his perspective, and gives me peace of mind.

Psalms 19:7

The law of the Lord is perfect, converting the soul: the testimony of the Lord is sure, making wise the simple.

Day 265

God comes into our presence, as we lift him up in praise; we get his total attention, when we thank him for his grace.

Psalms 22:3

But thou art holy, O thou that inhabitest the praises of Israel.

Day 266

Lord, it doesn't really matter what outside conditions may be, when I'm grounded in your word I thrive, with results that can be seen.

Jeremiah 17:8

For he shall be as a tree planted by the waters, and that spreadeth out her roots by the river, and shall not see when heat cometh, but her leaf shall be green; and shall not be careful in the year of drought, neither shall cease from yielding fruit.

Day 267

God wants to be involved in our lives, each and every part; but we have to trust his word, with all of our heart. We can't get distracted, with any other reports, or come to him only, as a last resort.

Jeremiah 29:13

And ye shall seek me, and find me, when ye search for me with all your heart.

Day 268

If we're not sure which way to go, the Holy Spirit will be our guide. He is like our spiritual compass, deposited on the inside.

Ezekiel 36:27

And I will put my spirit within you, and cause you to walk in my statutes, and ye shall keep my judgements, and do them.

Day 269

Food is important, but God's word feeds our soul. Jesus said feeding both of them, will make us complete and whole.

Luke 4:4

And Jesus answered him, saying, It is written, That man shall not live by bread alone, but by every word of God.

Day 270

With God's super on my natural I can do anything. I'm equipped and ready, for whatever life brings .

Philippians 4:13

I can do all things through Christ which strengtheneth me.

Day 271

Giving is an expression of God's love and care; but not if we feel pressured, or forced to share.

2 Corinthians 9:7

Every man according as he purposeth in his heart, so let him give; not grudgingly or of necessity: for God loveth a cheerful giver.

Day 272

Jesus is the promise kept, part of God's master plan; to make unconditional love and grace available to man.

John 1:14

And the Word was made flesh, and dwelt among us, (and we beheld his glory, the glory as of the only begotten of the Father,) full of grace and truth.

Day 273

We each have different gifts, that make us all unique Let's use them to work together, so Jesus they will seek.

1 Corinthians 12:12

For as the body is one, and hath many members, and all the members of that one body, being many, are one body: so also is Christ.

Day 274

Trust God more than money; it could be here today and gone tomorrow. When we trust in only what we have, it will eventually lead to sorrow. God will always be there for us; and said he'd never leave. He comes ready, willing and able to supply our every need.

1 Timothy 6:17

Charge them that are rich in this world, that they be not highminded, nor trust in uncertain riches, but in the living God, who giveth us richly all things to enjoy;

Day 275

There is nothing we can do, to deserve the gift of righteousness, the price was paid by Jesus, we need only accept and trust.

Titus 3:5

Not by works of righteousness which we have done, but according to his mercy he saved us, by the washing of regeneration, and renewing of the Holy Ghost;

Day 276

God doesn't make junk, we are masterpieces; one of a kind. When we realize how special we are to him, it will give us a new state of mind.

Psalms 139:14

I will praise thee; for I am fearfully and wonderfully made: marvellous are thy works; and that my soul knoweth right well.

Day 277

Following God's lead, will put us on the path to success. It affects every area of our lives, because God wants us to be blessed.

Isaiah 48:15

I, even I, have spoken; yea, I have called him: I have brought him, and he shall make his way prosperous

Day 278

People plot to bring down those, who want to do God's will, but their plans won't work, it will fall apart, and never be fulfilled.

Isaiah 54:17

No weapon that is formed against thee shall prosper; and every tongue that shall rise against thee in judgement thou shalt condemn. This is the heritage of the servants of the Lord, and their righteousness is of me, saith the Lord.

Day 279

The word of God is tried, tested and true; it gets results and accomplishes, what it's sent to do.

Psalms 12:6

The words of the Lord are pure words: as silver tried in a furnace of earth, purified seven times.

Day 280

God's plan to eliminate sin, which causes guilt and shame, gives us a brand new start, that's why Jesus came.

Jeremiah 33:8

And I will cleanse them from all their iniquity, whereby they have sinned against me; and I will pardon all their iniquities, whereby they have sinned, and whereby they have transgressed against me.

Day 281

Situations and people, will change from year to year, but God's promises never expire, lapse or disappear.

Mark 13:31

Heaven and earth shall pass away: but my words shall not pass away.

Day 282

God can handle what looks impossible to us, but he needs our unwavering trust.

Matthew 19:26

But Jesus beheld them, and said unto them, With men this is impossible; but with God all things are possible.

Day 283

Faith causes us to triumph, even before it is seen, it's the blueprint for success, and a life of victory.

1 John 5:4

For whatsoever is born of God overcometh the world: and this is the victory that overcometh the world, even our faith.

Day 284

When we believe only in what we can see, we miss out on the spiritual realm, that causes things to be.

2 Corinthians 4:18

While we look not at the things which are seen, but at the things which are not seen: for the things which are seen are temporal; but the things which are not seen are eternal.

Day 285

God knows the path in life we should take, when we let him guide us, there will be less mistakes.

Psalms 37:23

The steps of a good man are ordered by the Lord: and he delighteth in his way.

Day 286

Tell everyone about the joy that God's love brings, our hearts are so full, we can't help but sing.

1 Chronicles 16:9

Sing unto him, sing psalms unto him, talk ye of all his wondrous works.

Day 287

Make a decision to reach your goals God's way, and your destination will get closer with each passing day.

Psalms 37:5

Commit thy way unto the Lord; trust also in him; and he shall bring it to pass.

Day 288

Prayer is not just talking but involves listening too; it can change lives and situations, when we don't know what to do.

James 5:16

Confess your faults one to another, and pray one for another, that ye may be healed. The effectual fervent prayer of a righteous man availeth much.

Day 289

Don't be in a state of shock, when things looks upside down, have confidence that God will help, he'll turn it all around.

Joel 2:21

Fear not, O land; be glad and rejoice: for the Lord will do great things.

Day 290

I keep your word close to my heart, so when problems and temptations arise, I can stand on your promises with confidence, and not fall for the enemy's lies.

Psalms 119:11

Thy word have I hid in mine heart, that I might not sin against thee.

Day 291

We may not understand why things happen, and the way God wants us to go, but follow his lead, and trust his path, because your future he already knows.

Psalms 18:30

As for God, his way is perfect: the word of the Lord is tried: he is a buckler to all those that trust in him.

Day 292

Ask God for directions, and you won't get lost. He will always lead you to victory; trust is your only cost.

1 Samuel 30:8

And David enquired at the Lord, saying, shall I pursue after this troop? Shall I overtake them? And he answered him, Pursue: for thou shalt surely overtake them, and without fail recover all.

Day 293

Our only debt in life, is to love one another; to let God's love flow through us, and then out to others.

Romans 13:8

Owe no man any thing, but to love one another: for he that loveth another hath fulfilled the law.

Day 294

Being saved protects our spirit from the enemy's attack, and the word is our weapon, we can use to fight back.

Ephesians 6:17

And take the helmet of salvation, and the sword of the Spirit, which is the word of God.

Day 295

Seeking the Lord first, puts us on the path to success. There, we will find our purpose, and experience God's very best.

2 Chronicles 26:5

And he sought God in the days of Zechariah, who had understanding in the visions of God: and as long as he sought the Lord, God made him to prosper.

Day 296

Although with our leaders, we may not agree; pray for them, so that we can have peace.

1 Timothy 2:1-2

I exhort therefore, that, first of all, supplications, prayers, intercessions, and giving of thanks, be made for all men; For kings, and for all that are in authority; that we may lead a quiet and peaceable life in all godliness and honesty.

Day 297

God thinks and operates on a completely different level than man.
When we get to know him through his word, we begin to understand..

Isaiah 55:8

For my thoughts are not your thoughts, neither are your ways my
ways, saith the Lord.

Day 298

Be remembered for how you helped others, not for how much you
could buy, because we can't take anything with us, no matter how hard
we try.

1 Timothy 6:7

For we brought nothing into this world, and it is certain we can carry
nothing out.

Day 299

Self medication tries to replace heartache, hopelessness, and pain, but the peace is only temporary, and those feelings will remain. But Jesus came to free us, from all sickness and disease, whether physical, spiritual or emotional, he brings everlasting peace.

Luke 4:18

The Spirit of the Lord is upon me, because he hath anointed me to preach the gospel to the poor; he hath sent me to heal the brokenhearted, to preach deliverance to the captives, and recovering of sight to the blind, to set at liberty them that are bruised,

Day 300

Thank you Lord for your mercy, it will always last, your loving kindness towards me, no one can surpass.

1 Chronicles 16:34

O give thanks unto the Lord; for he is good; for his mercy endureth for ever.

Day 301

Thankful for all you've done for me, is how my day will start. I magnify your love and goodness when I praise you from my heart.

Psalms 86:12

I will praise thee, O Lord my God, with all my heart: and I will glorify thy name for evermore .

Day 302

God promises all throughout his word, that he will look out for us. Our only part in this relationship, is to simply trust.

Psalms 18:48

He delivereth me from mine enemies: yea, thou liftest me up above those that rise up against me: thou hast delivered me from the violent man.

Day 303

Faith connects us to what we believe, the word helps us visualize it, until it's received.

Hebrews 11:6

But without faith it is impossible to please him: for he that cometh to God must believe that he is, and that he is a rewarder of them that diligently seek him.

Day 304

The Lord wants to help us, but we have to make the first move. He has given us free will to decide, what kind of world we choose.

2 Chronicles 7:14

If my people, which are called by my name, shall humble themselves, and pray, and seek my face, and turn from their wicked ways; then will I hear from heaven, and will forgive their sin, and will heal their land.

Day 305

Just like God forgives us, we should forgive others. We all make mistakes, we are all sisters and brothers.

Matthew 6:14

For if ye forgive men their trespasses, your heavenly Father will also forgive you.

Day 306

We are God's children; he loves us all, his mercy picks us up, whenever we fall.

Psalms 145:9

The Lord is good to all: and his tender mercies are over all his works.

Day 307

Jesus answered any questions about Moses' law; loving God and each other, encompasses it all.

Matthew 22:37-40

Jesus said unto him, Thou shalt love the Lord thy God with all thy heart, and with all thy soul, and with all thy mind. This is the first and great commandment. And the second is like unto it, Thou shalt love thy neighbor as thyself. On these two commandments hang all the law and the prophets.

Day 308

When God is involved there is no need to doubt. Trust his loving-kindness to work things out.

Psalms 138:8

The Lord will perfect that which concerneth me: thy mercy, O Lord, endureth for ever: forsake not the works of thine own hands.

Day 309

Hopelessness will lead to depression and defeat, but with a glimmer of hope, any challenge can be beat.

Proverbs 13:12

Hope deferred maketh the heart sick, but when the desire cometh, it is a tree of life.

Day 310

There's no need to fear when adversity comes around, be confident in God's protection, he won't let us down.

Deuteronomy 31:6

Be strong and of a good courage, fear not, nor be afraid of them: for the Lord thy God, he it is that doth go with thee; he will not fail thee, nor forsake thee.

Day 311

Our hearts will reveal what we're all about, how we really think and feel, will eventually come out.

Proverbs 23:7

For as he thinketh in his heart, so is he: Eat and drink, saith he to thee, but his heart is not with thee.

Day 312

Before this world even came to be, God was around, and made all that we see.

Colossians 1:17

And he is before all things, and by him all things consist.

Day 313

When you don't see a way out, and the answers are unknown, remember God can make a difference, and you are not alone.

Daniel 3:25

He answered and said, Lo, I see four men loose, walking in the midst of the fire, and they have no hurt; and the form of the fourth is like the Son of God.

Day 314

God has unconditional love for us; a relationship is what he seeks. When we open our hearts to receive his love, our lives will be complete.

Jeremiah 24:7

And I will give them an heart to know me, that I am the Lord: and they shall be my people, and I will be their God: for they shall return unto me with their whole heart.

Day 315

No need to be afraid of anything; God will see us through whatever life brings.

Psalms 23:4

Yea, though I walk through the valley of the shadow of death, I will fear no evil: for thou art with me; thy rod and thy staff they comfort me.

Day 316

Righteousness is a gift, with many blessings to discover; those who reject the gift, end up with one problem after another.

Proverbs 15:6

In the house of the righteous is much treasure: but in the revenues of the wicked is trouble.

Day 317

When we are confident in God's love for us; nothing can shake our faith, and trust.

Romans 8:31

What shall we then say to these things? If God be for us, who can be against us.

Day 318

Don't give up or get discouraged when you make a mistake. Jesus will help you on your journey and progress you will make.

Philippians 1:6

Being confident of this very thing, that he which hath begun a good work in you will perform it until the day of Jesus Christ.

Day 319

Angels protect us, they are part of our inheritance. When we accept the gift of righteousness, our bodyguards are sent.

Hebrews 1:14

Are they not all ministering spirits, sent forth to minister for them who shall be heirs of salvation.

Day 320

When we trust God's direction, and not only what we see, he will lead us to blessings, peace and victory.

Psalms 32:8

I will instruct thee and teach thee in the way which thou shalt go: I will guide thee with mine eye.

Day 321

Praise is our weapon, that will boldly say, we will sing no matter what, because God will make a way.

Psalms 98:1

O Sing unto the Lord a new song; for he hath done marvellous things: his right hand and his holy arm, hath gotten him the victory.

Day 322

Jesus is the shepherd, that can lead us into grace; no matter where you come from, your religion or your race.

John 10:16

And other sheep I have, which are not of this fold; them also I must bring, and they shall hear my voice; and there shall be one fold, and one shepherd.

Day 323

The Old Testament teaches us what happened before, and gives us an appreciation of God's grace, that restores.

Romans 15:4

For whatsoever things were written aforetime were written for our learning, that we through patience and comfort of the scriptures might have hope.

Day 324

Faith is protection that guards our heart, it defends us from the enemy's devious plots.

Ephesians 6:16

Above all, taking the shield of faith, wherewith ye shall be able to quench all the fiery darts of the wicked.

Day 325

When you do a good deed, don't look for rewards and praise from man; do it to show God's love, and share as much as you can.

Ephesians 6:7

With good will doing service, as to the Lord, and not to men:

Day 326

Joy doesn't come from what you have, it comes from who you know. When you experience God's love and favor, it can't help but show.

Psalms 51:12

Restore unto me the joy of thy salvation; and uphold me with thy free spirit.

Day 327

How can we not forgive others, when we have been forgiven so much. Unforgiveness will isolate and harden our hearts, then we won't feel God's loving touch.

Mark 11:25

And when ye stand praying, forgive, if ye have ought against any: that your Father also which is in heaven may forgive you your trespasses.

Day 328

God's unconditional love is deep, and hard to understand, but once we experience it, we are complete, that is his master plan.

Ephesians 3:19

And to know the love of Christ, which passeth knowledge, that ye might be filled with all the fulness of God.

Day 329

Jesus paid the price for our sins, and put himself in our place. His sacrifice bridged the gap between God, and the human race.

1 Timothy 2:5

For there is one God, and one mediator between God and men, the man Christ Jesus.

Day 330

God wants a relationship with us, we don't have to be on our own. He wants to be part of our everyday lives, and to know we are not alone.

1 Timothy 2:4

Who will have all men to be saved, and to come unto the knowledge of the truth.

Day 331

Lord help me to think before I speak; let my words strengthen others, not make them weak.

Psalms 141:3

Set a watch, O Lord, before my mouth; keep the door of my lips.

Day 332

Our soul is worth more, than what the world can give, because how we think and feel, determines the life we live.

Mark 8:36

For what shall it profit a man, if he shall gain the whole world, and lose his own soul.

Day 333

We can overcome any obstacle and have the victory we seek, because believing and trusting God, makes us strong not weak.

Romans 8:37

Nay, in all these things we are more than conquerors through him that loved us.

Day 334

Fighting against the will of God, is a battle you will lose. Your life will be harder, and full of struggles, because of the side you choose.

Acts 5:39

But if it be of God, ye cannot overthrow it; lest haply ye be found even to fight against God.

Day 335

Don't be concerned with the negative words of a person that doesn't believe. Their advice won't work , there'll be no results, and nothing will be achieved.

Psalms 33:10

The Lord bringeth the counsel of the heathen to nought: he maketh the devices of the people of none effect.

Day 336

God can be trusted, he always keeps his word; his promises are real, no matter what you have heard.

Psalms 89:34

My covenant will I not break, nor alter the thing that is gone out of my lips.

Day 337

When we realize how much God loves us, its easy to spread the word. I'll tell of your grace and mercy, so your message will always be heard.

Psalms 34:1

I will bless the Lord at all times: his praise shall continually be in my mouth.

Day 338

The Holy Spirit is our teacher, guide and protection. He helps us stay on course, and pointed in the right direction.

John 14:26

But the Comforter, which is the Holy Ghost, whom the Father will send in my name, he shall teach you all things, and bring all things to your remembrance, whatsoever I have said unto you.

Day 339

Jesus is an extension of God, that men have seen with their eyes. He came to reunite us back to the Father, and defeat the father of lies.

John 10:30

I and my Father are one.

Day 340

God's mercy gives us a brand new start each and every day. He forgives and forgets all of our mistakes, and in the past they will stay.

Lamentations 3:22-23

It is of the Lord's mercies that we are not consumed, because his compassions fail not. They are new every morning: great is thy faithfulness.

Day 341

Give glory to God when he does something; you couldn't get done before. It demonstrates his power and ability, to bless us and open doors.

Mark 12:11

This was the Lord's doing, and it is marvellous in our eyes.

Day 342

Our Father guides us to a life of peace, not stress. In his presence there is provision, safety and rest.

Psalms 23:1-2

The Lord is my shepherd; I shall not want. He maketh me to lie down in green pastures; he leadeth me beside the still waters.

Day 343

When we think we can handle things on our own, it usually gets worse, and we feel so alone. Self centeredness is a dangerous place to be, it can lead to unhappiness and conceit.

Proverbs 16:18

Pride goeth before destruction, and an haughty spirit before a fall.

Day 344

Trusting God gives us strength, that will see us through, it kicks in when there's nothing more we can do.

Isaiah 40:31

But they that wait upon the Lord shall renew their strength; they shall mount up with wings as eagles; they shall run, and not be weary; and they shall walk, and not faint.

Day 345

Working for God should be a simple task; share the love he gives us, without being asked. Religion is man's attempt to work and be busy, but it's all for show and not at all necessary.

Colossians 3:23

And whatsoever ye do, do it heartily, as to the Lord, and not unto men.

Day 346

Those who take advantage, and cheat to succeed; will lose it to someone who will bless them that need.

Proverbs 28:8

He that by usury and unjust gain increaseth his substance, he shall gather it for him that will pity the poor.

Day 347

When you have the Lord fighting on your side, the enemy will retreat and hide.

Deuteronomy 3:22

Ye shall not fear them: for the Lord your God he shall fight for you.

Day 348

With you Lord, no obstacle gets the best of me. I can do super natural things; victory I see.

Psalms 18:29

For by thee I have run through a troop; and by my God have I leaped over a wall.

Day 349

Knowing the word of God will empower our soul, we'll see how awesome God is, as his blessings unfold.

Proverbs 24:14

So shall the knowledge of wisdom be unto thy soul: when thou hast found it, then there shall be a reward, and thy expectation shall not be cut off.

Day 350

God gives good judgement and peace, as an inheritance to his children. He also gives them wealth and riches, that the unbelievers are building.

Ecclesiastes 2: 26

For God giveth to a man that is good in his sight wisdom, and knowledge, and joy: but to the sinner he giveth travail, to gather and to heap up, that he may give to him that is good before God. This also is vanity and vexation of spirit.

Day 351

Believing and trusting God, is all that he asks. Our battle is to stay in faith, when it's not an easy task.

2 Timothy 4:7

I have fought a good fight, I have finished my course, I have kept the faith.

Day 352

Jesus destroyed the barrier between God and every man. He gives us access to all the blessings, the enemy tried to ban.

Ephesians 2:14

For he is our peace, who hath made both one, and hath broken down the middle wall of partition between us;

Day 353

Sometimes angels walk among us, to help us stay on course, they encourage us not to be afraid, by reminding us that God is our source.

Hebrews 13:2

Be not forgetful to entertain strangers: for thereby some have entertained angels unawares.

Day 354

Make God's word a part of your life, it's not just any book. When you need answers and directions, you will know just where to look.

2 Timothy 2:15

Study to shew thyself approved unto God, a workman that needeth not be ashamed, rightly dividing the word of God.

Day 355

Sometimes we get it wrong, because of what we don't do. Let's not wait for someone else to step up, God can make a difference with you.

James 4:17

Therefore to him that knoweth to do good, and doeth it not, to him it is sin.

Day 356

God can do more than we could ever think of or dream, but he needs us to trust him, and to simply believe.

Ephesians 3:20

Now unto him that is able to do exceeding abundantly above all that we ask or think, according to the power that worketh in us,

Day 357

Beware of people who say they know God, but their actions and words don't agree. They may look like church folks on the outside but in their lives no results will you see.

2 Timothy 3:5

Having a form of godliness, but denying the power thereof: from such turn away.

Day 358

When we can't make up our mind, to go to the left or right, don't expect to get anywhere; there's no destination in sight.

James 1:8

A double minded man is unstable in all his ways

Day 359

Amazing things happen, when we assemble to give God praise. His presence is felt, we feel right at home, and our worries just drift away.

Psalms 35:18

I will give thee thanks in the great congregation: I will praise thee among much people.

Day 360

When times are tough, those who trust God, will not be affected. He'll make a way, where there seems to be none; no lack will be detected.

Isaiah 58:11

And the Lord shall guide thee continually, and satisfy thy soul in drought, and make fat thy bones: and thou shall be like a watered garden, and like a spring of water, whose waters fail not.

Day 361

Life with you Lord, is filled with all kinds of treasures and benefits. Under your protection, mercy and grace, I look young, because there's no stress.

Psalms 103:4-5

Who redeemeth thy life from destruction; who crowneth thee with lovingkindness and tender mercies; who satisfieth thy mouth with good things; so that thy youth is renewed like an eagle's.

Day 362

Grace is undeserved favor and forgiveness, which some think we have to work for; but if we depend on our actions to earn it, then it is a gift no more.

Galatians 2:21

I do not frustrate the grace of God: for if righteousness come by the law, then Christ is dead in vain.

Day 363

When we answer God's call and trust him, he has many blessings in store. He has taken some wealth from the unbeliever, and delivered it to our door.

Isaiah 45:3

And I will give thee the treasures of darkness, and hidden riches of secret places, that thou mayest know that I, the Lord, which call thee by thy name, am the God of Israel.

Day 364

Since God saved Shadrach, Meshach, and Abednego from the burning fire, he can deliver us from any situation, it doesn't matter how dire.

Daniel 3:17

If it be so, our God whom we serve is able to deliver us from the burning fiery furnace, and he will deliver us out of thine hand O king.

Day 365

Jesus paid the price for my sin, and grace has made me free, but my actions still have consequences, which may not be good for me.

1 Corinthians 10:23

All things are lawful for me, but all things are not expedient: all things are lawful for me, but all things edify not.